Jewish
Worship

by Claudia Setzer

Anti-Defamation League of B'nai B'rith
823 United Nations Plaza
New York, N.Y. 10017

Jewish Worship

by Claudia Setzer

The Hebrew Bible is evidence of spontaneous and heartfelt prayer by Jews from the most ancient times: Moses and the children of Israel exalt God; Jeremiah petitions Him; Jonah, in the belly of the big fish, cries out to Him; the psalms praise Him. Throughout the ages, Jews have acknowledged prayer as a vital part of their daily life.

This publication describes the practices of those Jews who see tradition as guiding the form and function of their worship. Jewish religious observance varies widely, whether in observing dietary laws or the Sabbath. The chief point of departure is one's orientation toward Jewish law or *halacha*. (*Halacha* comes from the verb "to walk," and can be roughly translated as "the way" in which one should walk through life.) Jewish law is a system which permeates every aspect of life. Orthodox, Conservative, Reform and Reconstructionist groups have different interpretations of the significance of the *halacha*. They differ on how much authority they give to the Torah, to the rabbis of the Talmud, and to the medieval codes of Jewish law.

For the Orthodox, the authority is absolute; for the Reform, they are considered traditional, rather than binding law. Conservative Judaism tries to remain true to the process of Jewish law, but also to respond to the demands of modern life. Reconstructionist theory rejects certain ideas, such as the concept of the Chosen People, while holding on to other aspects of tradition. (Their services most closely resemble the Conservatives.) These attitudes affect the type of worship a group will have, especially, who may do what within worship.

Even the terms Othodox, Conservative, and Reform are merely umbrella terms. Within the Orthodox group there are a number of Hasidic communities, transplanted European groups which revere particular leaders. There are many Jews who defy categorization; there are those who would define themselves as secular Jews. It is best to view Judaism as a continuum, with the fundamentalists and strictly observant on one end and the completely secular on the other.

While we have tried to cover the diversity within modern Judaism, our characterization here will not always include those on the far ends of the continuum.

THE SYNAGOGUE

> "The way of the recluse, the exclusive concern with personal salvation, piety in isolation from the community is an act of impiety."
>
> Abraham Joshua Heschel,
> *Man's Quest for God*, p. 45

While any Jew may pray in solitude, in order to have communal prayer ten adult Jews* are required, including one able to lead the group in worship. Public worship need not take place in a synagogue. A service may be held anywhere ten Jews are gathered. Flying to Israel, one will probably witness a group gathered in the aisles for the morning service. Nevertheless, one can hardly overestimate the role which the synagogue has played in Jewish survival.

The synagogue building has also been a focus of Jewish artistic expression. Synagogue architecture takes many forms. A synagogue may be a magnificent building on New York's Fifth Avenue or a tiny *shtiebel* (literally a "little house"). Some Jewish symbol will usually appear on the outside, such as a *Magen David* (Shield of David), as well as the name of the congregation or a phrase from the Scriptures.

Jews did not always worship in synagogues. Initially they performed their religious obligations before the Ark of the Law, which was built to house the holy tablets of the Ten Commandments. The Ark was portable and accompanied the Israelites as they traveled to the Promised Land. After they settled in the land of Israel, King Solomon built a magnificent temple on Mount Zion in Jerusalem, with a special room set aside for the Ark.

The Jews worshiped in Solomon's Temple for about 350 years, until 586 B.C.E. In that year, Nebuchadnezzar, the king of Babylonia, made war on the Jews, looting and destroying the Temple. The Jews lost not only their place of worship, but their homeland. Many were carried off as captives to Babylonia. This period in Jewish history is known as "the Babylonian Exile."

By the time of the Exile, the Jews had already developed many religious observances: the Sabbath, holy days, and festivals. They refused to abandon them in the alien land of Babylonia. Seeing God's dominion as transcending national or political boundaries, Jews broke away from the customary worship of "national deities." Deprived of their Temple and the Holy Ark, they created new ways to practice their faith. They began to meet in each other's homes on Sabbaths and holy days to sing the psalms of the Temple. They read and discussed the holy scrolls they had salvaged from Jerusalem. They prayed for the time when they could return. (Today, no Jewish service is complete without mention of the special place of Zion and Jerusalem in the history of the Jewish people.) When the gatherings became too large for private homes, Jews built special halls for their meetings.

The Jews were permitted to return to Jerusalem after about 50 years of exile. They began to build a new temple on Mt. Zion, but continued the study meetings they had begun in Babylonia. These sessions of prayer and study of the holy writings became so popular that Jews began to congregate on Mondays

---

*Traditionally, only men have been counted. Today, all Reform, Reconstructionist, and many Conservative congregations include women in the quorum. Othodox congregations still only count adult males.

and Thursdays as well as the Sabbath. Soon, services were held daily and the Temple itself had a special place for these meetings.

The site for these gatherings was called a *Bet Knesset* (house of gathering), which the Greeks translated into *synagogue* (a gathering place). Although the Temple was still regarded as the House of the Lord, the Jews established many synagogues throughout the land of Israel. In fact, it was in the synagogues that Jesus preached to his fellow Jews.

By the time of Jesus and Paul, the synagogue was serving many functions. It was a place to study the Law and the Prophets. It was a community center for public meetings. It was used for the distribution of funds to the poor and for the shelter and care of strangers. Like the Temple, the synagogue became securely established as a necessary part of Jewish life.

In the year 70 C.E., six hundred years after the Jews had returned from Babylonia, the Temple was again destroyed. The Romans razed it and drove many Jews into exile or captivity. The synagogue was crucial in holding the Jews together during this crisis. It became the repository of God's word, and in it Jews felt close to Him.

Today's synagogue also serves as a gathering place for the Jews of the community, and many activities take place there. It bears some similarities to the ancient synagogue. Attached to the right-hand doorpost of its entrance is the *mezuzah*, a small roll of parchment in a case. The *mezuzah* is also found on the doorposts of Jewish homes. The parchment includes the Biblical verses in Hebrew from Deuteronomy 6:4-9.

Worshipers face Jerusalem. In American synagogues, the Ark will be on the eastern wall of the Sanctuary, while in India it will be on the western wall.

In a central spot in the sanctuary is a raised platform which contains the Ark. Here, the scrolls of the Torah are stored. The Ark and the richly embroidered curtain that covers it derive from the Tabernacle of Biblical days. There are a number of decorative and symbolic figures around the Ark. Often, two tablets with Hebrew letters, abbreviations for the Ten Commandments, hang above the Ark. Above the Ark hangs a *Ner Tamid*, an Eternal Light, to fulfill the Biblical injunction:

> You shall further instruct the Israelites to bring you clear oil of beaten olives for lighting, for kindling lamps regularly. Aaron and his sons shall set them up in the Tent of Meeting, outside the curtain which is over the Pact, [to burn] from evening to morning before the Lord. It shall be due from the Israelites for all time, throughout the ages.
>
> Exodus 27:20-21

When the Ark is opened, one sees the scrolls of the Torah, dressed in rich fabric and with exquisite silver crowns and breastplate. When the crowns are removed, two rollers or handles are seen. The ends of the parchment on which the Torah is written are attached to these rollers. By turning the rollers, the scroll is opened and closed.

Torah scrolls are handmade and written by a *sofer*, a scribe. A *sofer* must have training for his labor of devotion. He must follow very specific rules about margins, lines and the number of letters on each line. The parchment itself is

8

carefully made. Only the skins of *kosher* (ritually fit) animals are used. They are treated with chemicals to increase their durability and sewn together with dried tendons.

The Torah consists of the five books of Moses, the Pentateuch. A specific portion is chanted at each Torah reading. During the course of a year, the entire Torah will be read. It is chanted using an ancient system of muscial notation called *trope*.

The unique development of public study as worship, a concept started by Ezra the Scribe in the fifth century B.C.E., has since become basic to worship for many other religions.

There will probably also be two seven-branched candelabra on the dais. These *menorot* (singular, *menorah*) remind the congregation of the candelabrum used in the Temple in Jerusalem two millennia ago.

THE PRAYERS

"Which is the service of the heart? You must say, it is prayer."

Babylonian Talmud, Ta'anit 2a

The *siddur*, or prayer book, is a relatively new invention in Jewish life. The Hebrew Bible contains many forms of prayer: petition, confession, praise, thanksgiving. They indicate a belief that God exists and is interested in our welfare. He both hears and answers human beings. But there is no evidence of a fixed set of prayers employed by the Israelites.

Many of Judaism's basic liturgical units stem from the Mishnaic and Talmudic period (about 1-600 C.E.), though the actual wording and arrangement of many of the prayers were not finalized until a later period. Prayers were recited from memory and the rabbis resisted the writing down of prayers and blessings.

The first written prayer book, compiled by Rav Amram Gaon in Babylonia (present-day Iraq) at the request of the Spanish Jewish community, did not appear until the ninth century C.E. It contained prayers that had been transmitted orally for millennia. Other versions followed and today there are various prayer books in use by Jewish communities which may vary along ethnic, ritual and philosophical lines. Essentially, however, these prayer books follow the same format and include the same prayers.

Certain prayers are basic to Judaism and are found in all prayer books. The oldest is the *Shema* (literally, "hear"): "Hear, O Israel! The Lord is our God, the Lord alone," Deuteronomy 6:4, and the paragraph that follows it, Deuteronomy 6:5-9 and Deuteronomy 11:13-21. The declaration of belief is central to both morning and evening services.

The other basic part of the service is the *Amidah*, which means "standing," since that is how the prayer is recited. It is also called the *Shemoneh Esreh*, meaning "eighteen," since it was originally eighteen blessings (one was later added). The blessing, or *bracha* is the fundamental unit of Jewish prayer. It begins with the formula,

"Baruch attah, Adonai" ("Blessed [Praised] are You, Lord . . .") and then supplies an attribute of God, "who heals the sick," "who hears prayer," "who raises the dead," etc. Within a service, *berakot*, (blessings), begin and end larger prayers. The recitation of *berakot*, is not restricted to a service. They are recited for any number of instances where God's role in everyday life is recalled, e.g., before one eats an apple, when one sees a rainbow, when one sees a wise person, etc.

Probably the best-known prayer, even to the unschooled, is the *Kaddish*, the sanctification of God's name. It is thought of as a mourner's prayer, since it is recited in memory of a dead relative. The prayer, however, focuses on God, not on the relative. There is no mention of death in the *Kaddish*. There are three other forms of the *Kaddish* besides the one for mourners. They vary slightly in wording and act as divisions between parts of the service, closing one part of the service and beginning a new one. All versions of the *Kaddish* praise God's transcendent glory and greatness, noting the inability of human language to adequately praise Him.

The *Alenu*, a concluding prayer, expresses God's sovereignty. It is extremely

old and may have been composed before the destruction of the Temple in 70 C.E.

Adon Olam("Eternal Lord"), a popular liturgical hymn from the early medieval period, is frequently sung. There are many different melodies.

Aside from these basic prayers, there are a variety of others which praise, petition, and thank God. Many psalms and prayers express Jewish attachment to Jerusalem and the land of Israel.

The Torah service, a major event, takes place on the Sabbath, holidays, Mondays and Thursdays. The reverence for the Torah, the first five books of the Bible, and the obligation to study it are underscored by the pageantry surrounding its reading. The Torah scroll is ceremoniously removed from the ark and carried in procession around the synagogue. Its mantle is carefully removed and the scroll unrolled. Various people are given *aliyot*, i.e. called up to recite blessings and read from the Torah. Quite often, a Torah reader chants the day's selection as their agent. The Torah is divided into *parshiot*, or sections, which reflect the work of third-century Babylonian Jews. (The division of the Bible into chapters and verses was done by medieval Christians.) The Torah scroll is then rolled up again, tied with a sash, and covered with its decorated fabric cover and ornaments. A portion from the Prophets which is thematically related to the Torah reading is read. On Yom Kippur, for example, a day for fasting, the reading from the Prophets is Isaiah 57:14-58:14, which reminds us that God requires not just fasting but good deeds. The Torah is returned to the Ark, following another procession.

Prayer does not always take place in a public service. Jews are expected to pray every day and will often find themselves doing so at home and alone. The service said in private is somewhat shorter, but includes the *Shema* and the *Amidah*.

Traditionally, the prayers are said in Hebrew, with a few in Aramaic. But the *halacha* does not require they be said in any particular language.

Outline of a Regular Daily Morning Service (other than the Sabbath or a holiday)
1. Donning of the *talit* and *tefillin* (prayer shawl and phylacteries).
2. *Birchot HaShahar*: Early morning blessings, including Torah study.
3. *Pesukey DeZimrah*: Psalms of praise.
   Selections from Chronicles.
   Psalm 100, 145-150,
   Song at the Sea, Exodus 14:30-15:18.
4. Service proper:
   Shema and attendant *brachot*. *Amidah*: Eighteen blessings.
   Tahanun: Personal penitential prayer.
   Torah reading (on Mondays and Thursdays).
5. Concluding prayers:
   Psalms 145, 20.
   "A Redeemer will come to Zion": a rabbinic composition composed in Babylon during the Talmudic period (fourth through fifth centuries C.E.).
   Alenu.
   Daily psalm (originally said in the Second Temple).

FROM THE DAILY SERVICE

He is the eternal Lord, who reigned before any being had yet been created;

When all was done according to His will, already then His name was King.

And after all has ceased to be, still will He reign in solitary majesty—
He was, He is, and He shall be in glory.

And He is One, none other can compare to Him, or consort with Him;

He is without beginning, without end; to Him belongs power and dominion.

And He is my God, my living Redeemer, my Rock in time of trouble and distress;

He is my banner and my refuge, my benefactor when I call on Him.

Into His hands I entrust my spirit, when I sleep and when I wake; and with my spirit, my body also: the Lord is with me, I will not fear. (**Adon Olam/Eternal Lord**)

•

Praised are You, Lord our God, King of the universe who with wisdom fashioned the human body, creating openings, arteries, glands and organs, marvelous in structure, intricate in design. Should but one of them, by being blocked or opened, fail to function, it would be impossible to exist. Praised are you, Lord, healer of all flesh who sustains our bodies in wondrous ways.

•

These are the deeds which yield immediate fruit and continue to yield fruit in time to come; honoring parents; doing deeds of lovingkindness; attending the house of study punctually, morning and evening; providing hospitality; visiting the sick; helping the needy bride; attending the dead; probing the meaning of prayer; making peace between one person and another. And the study of Torah is the most basic of them all (because it leads to them all). (**Talmud**)

•

Praised are You, Lord our God, King of the universe who enables His creatures to distinguish between night and day. . . .who clothes the naked, who releases the bound. . . who strengthens the people Israel with courage, who crowns the people Israel with glory, who restores vigor to the weary.

•

We should always revere God, in private as in public. We should acknowledge the truth in our hearts and practice it in thought as in deed.

•

Halleluyah. . .The Lord rebuilds Jerusalem, gathers Israel's dispersed.

He heals the broken-hearted and binds up their wounds. He numbers all the stars and gives each one a name. . . . (Psalm 147)

•

May God be merciful to our fellow Jews who wander over sea and land or who suffer persecution and imprisonment. May He soon bring them relief from distress and deliver them from darkness to light, from subjugation to redemption. And let us say: Amen.

•

He being merciful, forgives iniquity, and does not destroy; frequently he turns his anger away, and does not stir up all His wrath.
O Lord, save us; may the King answer us when we call.

•

The Lord is near to all who call, to all who call upon Him in truth.

•

Praise the Lord, to whom our praise is due!
Praised be the Lord, to whom our praise is due, now and forever!

•

Deep is Your love for us, Lord our God, boundless Your tender compassion. . . . Open our eyes to Your Torah. . . . Bring us safely from the ends of the earth, and lead us in dignity to our holy land. . . .

•

Hear, O Israel! The Lord is our God. The Lord alone.
You shall love the Lord your God with all your heart and with all your soul and with all your might.
Take to heart these instructions which I charge you this day.
Impress them upon your children.
Recite them when you stay at home and when you are away, when you lie down and when you get up.
Bind them as a sign on your hand and let them serve as a symbol on your forehead;
inscribe them on the doorposts of your house and on your gates.

If you will earnestly heed the mitzvot that I give you this day, to love the Lord your God and to serve Him with all your heart and all your soul, then I will favor your land with rain at the proper season—rain in the autumn and rain in spring—and you will have an ample harvest of grain and wine and oil. I will assure abundance in the fields for your cattle. You will eat to contentment. Take care lest you be tempted to forsake God and turn to false gods in worship. For then the wrath of the Lord will be directed against you. He will close the heavens and hold back the rain; the earth will not yield its produce. You will soon disappear from the good land which the Lord is giving you. . . (**Shema Yisrael**/ **Hear O Israel**)

Praised are You, Lord our God and God of our ancestors, God of Abraham, of Isaac, and of Jacob, great, mighty, awesome, exalted God who bestows lovingkindness. Creator of all, You remember the pious deeds of our ancestors and will send a redeemer to their children's children because of Your loving nature.

•

You are the King who helps and saves and shields. Praised are You. Lord. Shield of Abraham . . . .

Your might, O Lord, is boundless. You give life to the dead; great is Your saving power.

You cause the wind to blow and the rain to fall.

Your lovingkindness sustains the living. Your great mercies give life to the dead. You support the falling, heal the ailing, free the fettered. Praised are You, Lord, Master of life and death . . . .

Accept the prayer of Your people Israel as lovingly as it is offered. Restore worship to Your sanctuary. May the worship of Your people Israel always be acceptable to You.

May we witness Your merciful return to Zion. Praised are You, Lord, who restores His Presence to Zion . . . .

May the Lord bless you and guard you.

May the Lord show you favor and be gracious to you.

May the Lord show you kindness and grant you peace . . . .

Grant peace to the world, with happiness, and blessing, grace, love, and mercy for us and for all the people Israel. Bless us, our Father, one and all, with Your light; for by that light did You teach us Torah and life, love and tenderness, justice, mercy, and peace. May it please You to bless Your people Israel in every season and at all times with Your gift of peace.

Praised are You, Lord, who blesses His people Israel with peace.

(**Amidah/Standing Prayer**)

•

My God, guard my tongue from evil, and my lips from speaking falsehood. May my soul be silent to those who insult me; be my soul lowly to all as the dust. Open my heart to thy Torah, that my soul may follow thy commands. Speedily defeat the counsel of all those who plan evil against me, and upset their design. Do it for the glory of thy name; do it for the sake of thy power; do it for the sake of thy holiness; do it for the sake of thy Torah. That thy beloved may be rescued, save with thy right hand and answer me. May the words of my mouth and the mediation of my heart be pleasing before thee. O Lord, my Stronghold and my Redeemer. May He who creates peace in His high heavens create peace for us and for all Israel. Amen.

•

Glorified and sanctified be God's great name throughout the world which He has created according to His will. May He establish His kingdom in your lifetime and during your days, and within the life of the entire house of Israel, speedily and soon; and say, Amen.

May His great name be blessed forever and to all eternity.

Blessed and praised, glorified and exalted, extolled and honored, adored and lauded be the name of the Holy One, blessed be He, beyond all the blessings and hymns, praises and consolations that are ever spoken in the world; and say, Amen.

May the prayers and supplications of the whole household of Israel be accepted by their Father who is in heaven; and say, Amen.

May there be abundant peace from heaven; and a good life, for us and for all Israel; and say, Amen.

He who creates peace in His celestial heights, may create peace for us and for all Israel; and say, Amen. (**Kaddish**)

FROM THE SABBATH SERVICE

The breath of all that lives praises You . . . .
Could song fill our mouth as water fills the sea
And could joy flood our tongue like countless waves,
Could our lips utter praise as limitless as the sky
And could our eyes match the splendor of the sun,
Could we soar with arms like eagle's wings,
And run with gentle grace, as the swiftest deer,
Never could we fully state our gratitude. For one ten-thousandth
of the lasting love,
Which is Your precious blessing, dearest God,
Granted to our ancestors and to us . . . .

•

We proclaim Your holiness on earth as it is proclaimed in heaven above. We sing the words of heavenly voices as recorded in Your prophet's vision:

Holy, holy, holy is the Lord of Hosts. The whole world is filled with His glory.

In thundering chorus, majestic voices resound, lifted toward singing seraphim and responding:

Praised is the glory of the Lord throughout the universe.

Throughout Your universe reveal Yourself, our King, and reign over us, for we await You. When will you reign in Zion? Let it be soon, in our time and throughout all time. May Your glory and holiness be apparent to all in Jerusalem, Your city, from generation to generation, eternally. May we see Your sovereignty, described in David's psalms which sing Your splendor.

The Lord shall reign through all generations; your God. Zion shall reign forever. Halleluyah . . . .

Moses rejoiced at the gift of his destiny when You declared him a faithful servant, adorning him with splendor as he stood in Your Presence atop Mount Sinai. Two tablets of stone did he bring down, inscribed with Shabbat observance.

17

THE RABBI AND THE CANTOR

"When a man is in trouble, do not cry out to the angel Michael or to the angel Gabriel, but to Me and I will answer immediately."

Jerusalem Talmud Berakhot 9:1, 12a

A rabbi does not possess any powers or responsibilities not given to the lay Jew. The rabbi does not intercede with God for the congregation nor perform any mystical rites. The rabbi is not needed to lead the public worship. He (or she) is primarily a teacher, though the rabbi's duties in the average synagogue are manifold. The rabbi may preach sermons, announce pages, lead a discussion on the Torah portion, counsel congregants, visit the sick, perform weddings, conduct funeral services, teach children and adults, and be an administrator.

In Talmudic times (up to the seventh century C.E.), the rabbinate was not a full-time vocation. Worshipers simply appointed the most respected scholar in the community. The scholar made a living like anyone else, perhaps as a blacksmith or sandal-maker. The scholar was called *rabbi*, which means teacher, as a mark of respect for his learning and piety. In the Gospels, Jesus is honored by his disciples with that title (Mk 9:5, Matt. 26:25).

While it is possible to receive private ordination, most train for the rabbinate today at seminaries. *Rabbi*, then, is a title for an ordained graduate of a Jewish seminary. The philosophies of the various institutions, and their orientation toward Jewish practice, are as varied as the many movements within Judaism today. Students usually begin rabbinical school after acquiring a college degree, though the more Orthodox-fundamentalist institutions do not require it. Students then embark on a four-to-six-year period of theological study. A rabbi is encouraged to marry and raise a family.

The other highly visible professional in the synagogue service is the cantor. Not every synagogue has one. Like the rabbi, the cantor is not absolutely necessary to the service. The cantor, or *hazzan*, chants the prayers and leads the congregation in worship. He (or she) may also read from the Torah.

(The Torah reader chants from the appropriate portion of the Pentateuch on the Sabbath, holidays, and Monday and Thursday mornings.) As with the rabbi, the position of cantor was originally an honorary one which later became a profession in itself. The education of the prospective cantor includes years of study of both Judaica and music.

The *shammes* corresponds to the Christian "sexton." He (or she) sees to the physical needs of the synagogue, such as lights, seating, and prayer books, as well as the technical aspect of the services. The *shammes* may also teach.

Women can now receive rabbinic ordination from Reform, Reconstructionist and Conservative theological seminaries. Prayer services in Reform, Reconstructionist and a growing number of Conservative synagogues are egalitarian: Women are counted for the *minyan* (quorum), they can lead in the prayers, read from the Torah scroll and in general fully participate in all aspects of the service. In some Orthodox communities, women have formed their own study/prayer groups in which they conduct all parts of the service.

One person may assume several of the above functions or they may be assumed by members of the congregation. Many small synagogues have no rabbi or cantor.

There are a number of honorary functions at each service. A congregant might be called up to the Torah to assist in the reading, lift up the Torah for the community to view, open or close the Ark where the Torah is kept, dress the Torah after its reading, or lead a responsive reading. Normally only those considered adults (males age 13 or over, females age 12 or over) are given these honors. In some congregations, only men have these privileges. In others, women may share some or all of these functions.

Although a rabbi or cantor may officiate at services, the congregation communes directly with God. Each Jew's relationship with God is unmediated.

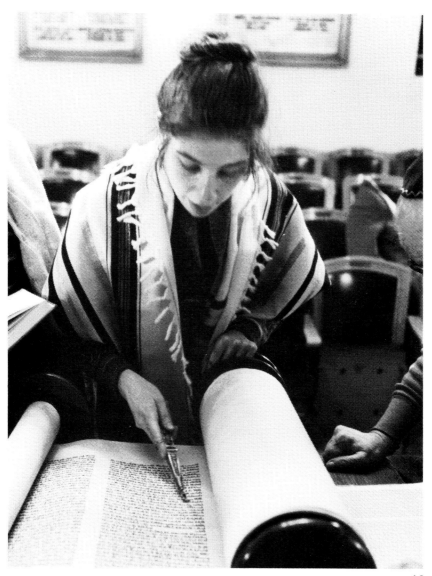

TIME FOR PRAYER

"When you pray, do not make your prayer a routine (or fixed form) act, but a plea for mercy and grace before God."

Pirke Avot (Ethics of the Fathers) 2:13

Traditional Judaism seeks a balance between spontaneity and formality in prayer. Certain prayers must be said at certain times, but some rabbis of the Jerusalem Talmud suggested that a new prayer be said every day to prevent prayer from becoming routine.

There are three daily services, or sets of prayers. The morning, afternoon, and evening services are recited seven days a week, in public or private. The morning service is the longest, and includes many preliminary psalms and blessings, the main body of the service, and a number of closing prayers. The afternoon service corresponds to the daily afternoon sacrifice in the Temple. The evening service is scaled down from the morning one, without the numerous preliminary and concluding prayers.

The liturgy for the Sabbath includes many psalms and verses which celebrate the Sabbath. Prayers which have a hint of sadness, like some petitions or confessions, are not said. Holidays have their individual prayers and customs, like the blowing of the *shofar*, (ram's horn) on Rosh Hashanah, the New Year, or dancing with the Torah on *Simhat Torah* (The Rejoicing of the Torah).

Certain rites of passage may take place in a synagogue, i.e., a circumcision, *Bar/Bat Mitzvah*, wedding or baby-naming. Since the *Bar/Bat Mitzvah* denote coming of age for carrying out the Torah's commandments, they are usually centered around a Torah service. The other life-cycle events have their own ceremonies and may take place without a service.

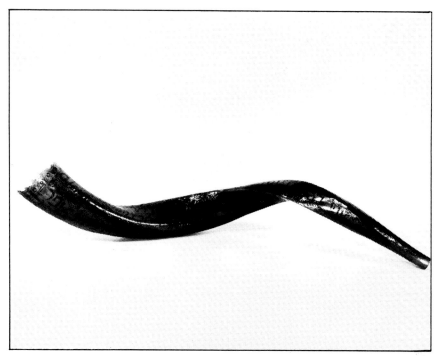

CEREMONIAL OBJECTS AND ACTIONS

"This is my God and I will glorify Him."

Exodus 15:2

There are certain ceremonial objects and distinctive actions which are unique to Jewish prayer.

In any Orthodox or Conservative synagogue, one will see all the men (and some of the women) wearing *kippot*, skull-caps or *yarmulkes*. The wearing of a head-covering is a Near Eastern way of showing respect and reverence before God. This is contrasted with the Western sign of respect, which is to uncover the head. The roots of this custom are blurred and the tradition is not clear about who should cover the head and when. But the present practice of wearing a *kippah* or hat, at least for prayer and study, has taken on the force of obligation for the observant Jew. Reform congregations do not require it. Traditionally, married women cover their heads at prayer.

If one attends a Sabbath or weekday morning service, one will also notice people wearing prayer shawls. The *talit* (shawl) is usually white and may have blue or black stripes or other decorations. It must be a four cornered garment and have *tzittzit*, (fringes), on each corner. The source of this custom is quite clear:

The Lord said to Moses as follows: "Speak to the Israelite people and instruct them to make for themselves fringes on the corners of their garments throughout the ages; let them attach a cord of blue to the fringe at each corner. That shall be your fringe; look at it and recall all the commandments of the Lord and observe them, so that you do not follow your heart and eyes in your lustful urge. Thus you shall be reminded to observe all My commandments and to be holy to your God."

Numbers 15:37-40

The primary reason for this—and indeed any ritual act—is to recall God's love and faithfulness and remind one of His commandments.

The larger garment, the *talit*, lends itself to many kinds of symbolism, e.g., the idea of being wrapped up and protected by God's presence. In some Orthodox synagogues, normally only married men wear the *talit*, while in Conservative ones all adult males do. Women are neither required nor forbidden to wear them and increasingly are choosing to do so. The Reform movement does not view the *talit* or *tzittzit* as obligatory, although some Reform Jews wear them.

On weekday mornings, *tefillin*, or phylacteries, are worn on the head and the "weak" hand and arm (i.e. the left arm if one is right handed). They are small leather boxes containing tiny pieces of parchment with portions of the Torah written on them. The wearing of *tefillin* for males is an injunction of Biblical origin:

"And so it shall be as a sign upon your hand as a symbol on your forehead that with a mighty hand the Lord freed us from Egypt."

Exodus 13:16, also Exodus 13:9, Deuteronomy 6:8, 11:18.

Since the *tefillin* are primarily a "sign," or reminder of God's care, and the Sabbath itself is considered such a sign, they are not worn on the Sabbath or most holidays. Reform Jews do not wear them. Some Conservative and Orthodox women

have begun to wear them. Jewish law does not require them to do so; neither does it prohibit it.

In addition to using special objects, the Jew moves in unique ways during prayer. The worshiper sways back and forth, bows, rises on tiptoes, takes three steps backward and forward, and cover the eyes. The praying individual hardly ever stands still. Jews do not kneel at prayer, however, except for the *Aleinu* on Yom Kippur. In part, these actions are simply reflections of Near Eastern manners, manners which show reverence before a monarch. Since Jews are beholden to the King of Kings, the Divine Presence, they retain these manners. Some of these movements aid concentration. They also reflect the idea that one praises God not just with words, but with one's whole body: "All my bones shall say, 'Lord, who is like You?' "   Psalm 35:10

SELECTED BIBLIOGRAPHY ON JEWISH WORSHIP

Donin, H., *To Pray as a Jew* (New York: Basic Books, 1980).
   Practical, elementary guide to the prayer book and synagogue service written from an Orthodox perspective.

Encyclopaedia Judaica (Jerusalem: Keter, 1972).
   See articles under "Liturgy," "Synagogue," and "Prayer."

Garfiel, E., *The Service of the Heart: A Guide to the Jewish Prayer Book* (New York/London: Th. Yoseloff, 1958).
   Examination of synagogue service and individual prayers from a historical perspective. Readable, does not require any background knowledge.

Heschel, A. J., *Man's Quest for God* (New York: Scribner, 1954).
   Collection of short meditations on the inner life. Poetic and theological in tone.

Jacobs, L., *Hasidic Prayer* (London: Routledge & Kegan Paul, 1972).
   For the reader with a special interest and some background in Hasidism, a study of the Hasidic masters' attitudes toward prayer.

Klein, I., *A Guide to Jewish Religious Practice* (New York: The Jewish Theological Seminary of America, 1979).
   Reference book on the legal particulars of Jewish prayer. Not for the beginner.

Millgram, A., *Jewish Worship* (Philadelphia: Jewish Publication Society, 1971).
   Broad-range, technical introduction for the educated lay person.

Petuchowski, J., *Understanding Jewish Prayer* (New York: Ktav, 1972).
   The first half of the book contains the author's remarks on the experience of worship and includes traditional sources. Second half is an anthology of essays on prayer by modern Jewish thinkers.

Rossel, S., *When a Jew Prays* (New York: Behrman, 1973).
   Developed for use in Hebrew schools, explains the basics of Jewish prayer in an engaging manner. Appropriate for 10-14-year-olds.

Siegel, R., Strassfeld, M., and Strassfeld, S., *The Jewish Catalog: A Do-It-Yourself Kit* (Philadelphia: Jewish Publications Society, 1973).

Strassfeld, M., and Strassfeld, S., *The Second Jewish Catalog* (New York: Jewish Publication Society, 1976).
   Introductory, readable collections of articles on a variety of Jewish topics. Both catalogs contain short articles on prayer and synagogue etiquette.

PRAYER BOOKS:

Ha-Siddur Ha-Shalem: The Daily Prayer Book (ed. P. Birnbaum; New York: Hebrew Publishing Co., 1977).
   A standard, Orthodox prayer book, which contains Hebrew and English translations.

Siddur Sim Shalom (ed. J. Harlow; New York: Rabbinical Assembly, 1985).
    The newest prayer book issued by the Conservative movement,
    contains an explanatory introduction, as well as prayers in Hebrew
    and English.
Shaarei Tefillah, The Gates of Prayer: The New Union Prayer Book (New York: Central
Conference of American Rabbis, 1975).
    The most recent version of the Reform movement's prayer book,
    contains prayers in Hebrew and English.

Photo Credits:

Cover: Torah Ark, Jerusalem, Lauros-Giraudon/Art Resource
Page 4: Touro Synagogue, National Landmark, Rhode Island
Page 7: (top) Florence, Italy synagogue, Colleziona Brogl/Art Resource
        (bottom) Touro Synagogue, Bruce Anspach, EPA/Art Resource
Page 9: Prayer service, Bill Aron
Page 10: Torah Scribe, Bill Aron
Page 12: Alain Keler, EPA/Art Resource
Page 19: Reading from Torah Scroll, Bill Aron
Page 20: Dancing with the Torah Scrolls on Simhat Torah,
        Bruce Anspach, EPA/ Art Resource
Page 21: Shofar (Ram's horn) The Jewish Museum/Art Resource
Page 23: Putting on Teffilin, Bill Aron
Page 24: Bag for Tallit, The Jewish Museum/Art Resource
Back Cover: Torah Pointer and Torah Scroll, The Jewish
            Museum/Art Resource

We wish to thank the publishers for the translations of the prayers
on pages 14-17

Siddur Sim Shalom, Edited, with translations by Rabbi Jules Harlow.
Published by the Rabbincal Assembly and the United Synagogue of
America, 1985.
Gates of Prayer: The New Union Prayerbook, Rabbi A. Stanley Dreyfus,
Chairman Liturgy Committee. Published by the Central Conference
of American Rabbis.

For further information on publications and audio-visual materials
about Jews, Judaism and Jewish-Christian relations, we invite the
reader to send for the catalogue, *Human Relations Materials for the
School, Church and Community* from the Anti-Defamation League of
B'nai B'rith.